YOU SHOULD MEET Jesse Owens

by Laurie Calkhoven

illustrated by Elizabet Vukovic

Ready-to-Read

Simon Spotlight
New York   London   Toronto   Sydney   New Delhi

SIMON SPOTLIGHT

An imprint of Simon & Schuster Children's Publishing Division

1230 Avenue of the Americas, New York, New York 10020

This Simon Spotlight edition January 2017

Text copyright © 2017 by Simon & Schuster, Inc.

Illustrations copyright © 2017 by Elizabet Vukovic

All rights reserved, including the right of reproduction in whole or in part in any form.

SIMON SPOTLIGHT, READY-TO-READ, and colophon are registered trademarks

of Simon & Schuster, Inc.

For information about special discounts for bulk purchases, please contact Simon & Schuster Special Sales at

1-866-506-1949 or business@simonanhdschuster.com.

Manufactured in the United States of America 1216 LAK

2 4 6 8 10 9 7 5 3 1

Library of Congress Cataloging-in-Publication Data

Names: Calkhoven, Laurie, author. | Vukovic, Elizabet, illustrator. Title: Jesse Owens / by Laurie Calkhoven ;

illustrated by Elizabet Vukovic. Description: Simon Spotlight /paperback edition.

New York : Simon Spotlight, [2017] | Series: You Should Meet | "Ready-to-Read." | Audience: Ages: 5-7.

Identifiers: LCCN 2016049021 (print) | LCCN 2016051498 (eBook) | ISBN 9781481480956 (pbk)

ISBN 9781481480963 (hc) | ISBN 9781481480970 (eBook) | ISBN 9781481480970 Subjects: LCSH: Owens,

Jesse, 1913-1980—Juvenile literature. | Track and field athletes—United States—Biography—Juvenile literature.

| African American track and field athletes—Biography—Juvenile literature.

Classification: LCC GV697.O9 C35 2017 (print) | LCC GV697.O9 (eBook) |

DDC 796.092 [B]—dc23 LC record available at https://lccn.loc.gov/2016049021

CONTENTS

Have you ever watched the Olympics and dreamed about winning a gold medal? Have you ever imagined running as fast as the wind or jumping so high that you touched the sky?

If so, you should meet Jesse Owens.

Jesse Owens had to help support his family when he was a child, so he worked in the cotton fields and shined shoes. But that didn't stop him from following his dream to become an Olympic track-and-field star.

Jesse went to the Olympics in Berlin, Germany, in 1936. The German government didn't believe that black people or Jewish people were as good as Germans. That didn't stop Jesse from proving them wrong and winning four gold medals.

If you like American heroes, then you should meet Jesse Owens!

Chapter 1
Alabama Cotton Fields

James Cleveland Owens was born on September 12, 1913, in Oakville, Alabama. He was the youngest of ten children. His family had very little money. During the winter, cold wind blew through the cracks in the walls of their house. J.C., as his family called him, was often sick.

J.C.'s grandparents had been slaves. His own parents were *sharecroppers*. That meant they lived on another farmer's land and gave that farmer part of their crops as payment. The whole family had to work.

When J.C. was seven years old, he was picking a hundred pounds of cotton a day. When he could, he walked the nine miles to and from the only school for black students. Black children and white children were not allowed to attend school together.

J.C.'s sister had moved to Cleveland, Ohio, and told the family that they could have a better life there. Soon the rest of J.C.'s family decided to move to Cleveland as well, where J.C.'s father got a job in a steel mill. Nine-year-old J.C. got on a train with his family and rode north.

making him the first track-and-field star in United States history to win four gold medals at the Olympics.

He was an Olympic hero.

Chapter 5
An Olympic Hero Comes Home

Jesse came home an Olympic champion, but life for black people in the United States hadn't changed.

New York City gave Jesse a ticker-tape parade on Broadway. But when Jesse and Ruth went to a fancy dinner in his honor, they had to use the elevator that the waiters and maids used.

"When I came back to my native country, after all the stories about Hitler, I couldn't ride in the front of the bus," Jesse said. "I had to go to the back door. I couldn't live where I wanted. I wasn't invited to shake hands with Hitler, but I wasn't invited to the White House to shake hands with the president, either."

Jesse had received many job offers while he was in Germany, but most of those dried up when he got home. He struggled to make a living. He and Ruth eventually had two more daughters, and Jesse did what he could for them. At one point, he even raced against horses to earn money. People said it was beneath him, but Jesse pointed out that he had to eat.

Change came slowly. In a 1950 Associated Press poll, Jesse was named the greatest track-and-field athlete of the previous fifty years.

The state of Illinois asked him to help promote athletics. He tried to inspire young people the way his coach, Charles Riley, had inspired him. Then Jesse traveled around the world for the US government to promote sports and democracy.

In 1976, Jesse was finally invited to the White House. President Gerald R. Ford gave Jesse the Presidential Medal of Freedom, the highest honor a civilian can

achieve. Jesse went on to win many more awards and continued to promote sports and the Olympics, until he died in 1980.

Jesse never stopped fighting for what he believed in. He never gave up on his dreams, and his passion, determination, and hard work made him a hero.

Now that you've met him, don't you think you can do the same?

BUT WAIT . . .

THERE'S MORE!

Turn the page to learn a little bit about history, the Olympics, and some cool track-and-field facts.

Historical Hurdles

Jesse Owens rose to fame in the face of
tragic events at home and abroad.

Jim Crow Laws

1877–1965

After the Civil War, the Southern United States
created laws known as Jim Crow laws. These
laws ensured that black people could not work,
live, or learn in the same places as white people.
The laws forced black people to use separate
bathrooms, park benches, schools, hospitals, lunch
counters, even water fountains. If black Americans
broke these laws, they faced violence, fines, and
imprisonment. The Jim Crow laws began long
before Jesse was born and
remained in effect
until he was more
than fifty years
old. The civil
rights movement
finally caused
Congress to
strike down
these laws in 1964
and 1965.

The Great Depression

1929–1939

When Jesse was sixteen years old, the Great Depression began. This was a time of severe poverty in North America and Europe. In the United States, companies closed, jobs disappeared, banks failed, and millions of families struggled to survive. At one time there were fifteen million people who wanted to work but could not find jobs. This time was particularly hard on black Americans. Previously, black people could find employment by taking low-paying jobs that white people would not take. Once the Depression began, white people would take any job available. Even some soup kitchens (places that serve free hot soup and other meals to people who can't afford food) refused to serve black men, women, and children. While the Great Depression ended when the United States entered World War II, the racism did not.

History of the Olympics

The Olympic Games started in ancient Greece in 776 BCE—that was more than two thousand years ago! Originally meant to celebrate the athletic abilities of young people, the Games also encouraged friendliness between the cities of Greece.

The ancient Olympic Games were held every four years while people were gathered for a religious festival. A group of all male athletes from around the country competed in different events—footraces, the long jump, the discus and javelin throws, wrestling, and chariot racing. The ancient Olympics continued for many centuries, until the Roman emperor Theodosius I banned them in the year 393 CE.

The Olympic Games began again more than fifteen hundred years later in 1896. After a visit to Greece, a French nobleman named Baron Pierre de Coubertin was  inspired to hold international Olympic Games. He hoped they would promote physical education around the world.

Women competed for the first time at the 1900 Games in Paris. Today, more than thirteen thousand athletes, male and female, from 204 different countries compete at the summer and winter Olympic Games. Athletes compete in fifty-six different sports and 406 events. The Games are held in a different city each time, in a special stadium built just for the Olympics.

After each event, the world watches as three medals are awarded. The athlete who finishes in third place receives the bronze medal. The athlete who finishes in second place receives the silver medal. Finally, the first-place winner receives the coveted Olympic gold medal. Out of thirteen thousand athletes, only a few get to "take home the gold."

• There are 8 running events in track: 100-meter sprint, 200-meter sprint, 400-meter sprint, 800-meter sprint, 1500-meter sprint, marathon, hurdles, and relays. (Women and men compete separately.)

• The shortest race is the 100-meter sprint. The longest is a 26.2-mile race called a *marathon*.

• It takes the average person about 4 ½ hours to run a marathon. The current world record for the fastest marathon is 2 hours, 2 minutes, and 57 seconds.

• A *triathlon* is a long race made up of 3 events: swimming, bicycling, and running.

• A *decathlon* is a contest made up of 10 events: 3 running races, hurdles, javelin and discus throws, shot put, pole vault, high jump, and long jump.

- The first recorded ancient Olympic event was a 600-foot-long footrace called the *stade*. It was the length of the stadium.

- A lap around today's modern outdoor track is a distance of 400 meters, or about 1,312 feet.

- Competitive sprinters train 20 hours a week.

- The average person can jump anywhere between 1 foot and 1 foot, 8 inches high. The highest high jump ever recorded was 8 feet, .45 inches.

- The length of an average person's jump is anywhere from 5 feet, 7 ½ inches to 7 feet, 6 ½ inches. The longest long jump ever recorded was 29 feet, 4.36 inches.

- In a 4 x 100 relay race, each team has 4 runners, and the teams compete against one another. Each runner runs a 100-meter sprint before passing the baton to the next teammate.

Now that you've met Jesse, what have you learned?
Take this quiz and find out!

1. In which state was Jesse born?
a. Ohio   b. Alabama   c. Iowa

2. Coach Riley told Jesse to run like the track was on fire. What does that mean?
a. To plant his feet on the ground   b. To pick up his feet quickly
c. To stay low to the ground

3. Where did Jesse live when he earned the nickname the "Buckeye Bullet"?
a. Alabama   b. Olympia   c. Ohio

4. Jesse Owens tied a world record on May 25, 1935. He also beat how many world records that day?
a. three   b. four   c. five

5. Where were the 1936 Olympic Games held?
a. Greece   b. Russia   c. Germany

6. Which political party did Adolf Hitler lead?
a. Communist   b. Nazi   c. Unionist

7. What did Jesse struggle with after the Olympics?
a. employment   b. fame   c. loneliness

8. When was Jesse invited to the White House?
a. 1936   b. 1950   c. 1976

Answers: 1. b 2. b 3. c 4. a 5. c 6. b 7. a 8. c